THE NEW PLANT LIBRARY

# LILIES

# THE NEW PLANT LIBRARY

# LILIES

### ANDREW MIKOLAJSKI

Consultant: Christine Skelmersdale
Photography by Peter Anderson

LORENZ BOOKS

First published in 1998 by Lorenz Books

© Anness Publishing Limited 1998

Lorenz Books is an imprint of Anness Publishing Limited
Hermes House, 88-89 Blackfriars Road, London SE1 8HA

This edition published in the USA by Lorenz Books, Anness Publishing Inc.,
27 West 20th Street, New York, NY 10011; (800) 354-9657

This edition distributed in Canada by Raincoast Books
8680 Cambie Street, Vancouver, British Columbia V6P 6M9

ISBN 1 85967 634 0

A CIP catalogue record for this book is available from the British Library

*Publisher* Joanna Lorenz
*Senior Editor* Cathy Marriott
*Designer* Michael Morey
*Photographer* Peter Anderson

Printed and bound in Hong Kong / China

1 3 5 7 9 10 8 6 4 2

■ HALF-TITLE PAGE
'Royal Class'
■ FRONTISPIECE
'Wall Street'
■ TITLE PAGE
'Moneymaker'

■ LEFT
*L. martagon*
■ OPPOSITE LEFT
Royal Gold Group
■ OPPOSITE RIGHT
'Vico Queen'

# Contents

# Introduction

*A*mong the most stately and elegant of garden plants, lilies have excited much attention from botanists, poets and artists. The lily has acquired a unique resonance in many cultures, matched only by the rose. Whether planted in drifts in light woodland, in the herbaceous or mixed border, or in containers on the patio, lilies can be guaranteed to make an impact. Some have bold, showy flowers that can be intoxicatingly scented, while others have nodding flowers of more subtle appeal. Whatever the conditions in your garden, there is a lily to thrive there. They can be grown in beds, in pots, even in the greenhouse or conservatory. This book shows you how to grow and care for these rewarding plants, and illustrates some of the most beautiful species and hybrids now available.

■ RIGHT
Among the most desirable of summer bulbs, lilies make an impact in a variety of situations.

■ RIGHT
**Many modern hybrids come in a range of rich colours and combine hardiness with vigour.**

with the Virgin (hence the common name Madonna lily), its white petals symbolizing her purity, though it is worth noting that the flower was also sacred to the goddess Juno, the Roman queen of heaven.

In the second half of the 16th century, many bulbs and tubers were imported into Europe from Constantinople, including crown imperials, hyacinths, tulips and lilies. They became popular in European gardens, usually grown in geometrically shaped beds in the Italian or Islamic fashion. Two important Renaissance herbals speak of lilies: Gerard's *Herball* (1597) and Parkinson's *Paradisus terrestris* (1629). In 1597 the Italian horticulturist Agostino del Riccio also published his treatise, *Del giardino di un re*, with a suggested planting that includes 12 different lilies.

The opening up of the Americas led to further discoveries, and plant collecting became a serious pursuit. There was two-way traffic across the Atlantic. In the 17th century, Dutch settlers took their favourite plants with them, including lilies, while one of the most significant introductions from North America was the American turkscap lily, *L. superbum*, sent to England in 1735 by John Bartram (1699–1777), the first

American-born botanist.

Louis XIV was an *aficionado* of lilies, and the flower beds at Versailles included some of the new North American imports, including *L. canadense*, introduced in 1620. They were grown in blocks, the beds edged with clipped box (*Buxus*), but in the 18th century it became fashionable to

plant in serried ranks: pinks were used at the front of the bed for edging, with shorter growing herbaceous perennials and spring bulbs behind. At the back, lilies were planted beside other taller plants such as golden rod (*Solidago*), hollyhocks and evening primroses (*Oenothera*).

In the 19th century, the Empress

■ LEFT
*L. speciosum,* from the Far East, has several variants including var. *rubrum* shown here.

Josephine (1763–1814) planted one of the most famous of all contemporary gardens at Malmaison, Hauts-de-Seine, and the botanical artist Pierre Joseph Redouté illustrated many of her plants, the lilies appearing in his most sumptuous volume, *Les Liliacées.*

Later that century, the English gardening writer Shirley Hibberd (1825–90) advocated a less formal approach to planting than bedding out. He proposed a herbaceous border that included lilies alongside other hardy perennials such as hostas, daylilies (*Hemerocallis*), delphiniums and anemones. The Irish writer and gardener William Robinson (1838–1935) took the idea further and developed "wild", or more naturalistic planting. It became popular to plant areas of woodland

with lilies that are at home in such conditions alongside other woodland plants such as anemones and ferns.

The 19th and early 20th centuries constitute the great era of plant hunting, when there were many notable introductions. *L. mona-delphum* arrived from the Caucasus around the end of the 18th century. A little later came the Himalayan *L. nepalense.* One of the most significant introductions was *L. speciosum* (found in Japan, east China and Taiwan), which arrived in Europe in 1830, and is valued for its vigour, scent and late flowering. *L. auratum* was introduced from Japan in 1862, though it is possible that it was already known in France in the 17th century. *L. davidii* was found in western China in the 19th century by the missionary and naturalist Père David. Other

Chinese species later introduced to cultivation include *L. duchartrei.* *L. hansonii* arrived from Korea (the plant is also found in Siberia and Japan). *L. henryi* was an important introduction from central China that has been widely used for hybridizing. *L. sargentiae* arrived from western China at the start of the 20th century.

Probably the most significant introduction, however, was that of *L. regale* by the plant hunter Ernest H. Wilson from Hupeh in China in 1910. Wilson broke his leg in an avalanche while on the expedition, and brought back bulbs of the species only in the teeth of extraordinary adversity. Despite its restricted distribution in the wild, this has proved one of the most adaptable of all lilies and has deservedly become one of the most widely grown.

Crosses made in Holland and Germany in the first half of the 19th century between *L. candidum* and *L. chalcedonicum* resulted in *L. x testaceum.* Towards the end of the 19th century, Mrs R.O. Backhouse of Hereford in England developed a strain of hybrids using *L. martagon* and *L. hansonii.* Of these, 'Mrs R.O. Backhouse' is still available. In the USA in the 1920s, the Bellingham

■ BELOW
'Karen North' is one of a number of hybrids raised in Scotland in the 20th century.

recent development has been the breeding of dwarf lilies that are especially suited to pot culture. Formerly, dwarf lilies were produced by growing the plants in pots and treating them with growth-inhibiting chemicals. However, the discovery of a mutation of *L. auratum* led to the breeding of lilies that are genetically dwarf. Many have been raised in the USA, and these are becoming increasingly popular in Europe and elsewhere.

Hybrids were raised in Bellingham, Washington, 'Shuksan' being particularly noteworthy. Jan de Graaff at his farm in Oregon, northwest USA, did much further breeding to widen the colour range, which now includes yellow to orange and red. De Graaff also produced the Olympic Hybrids, 'Green Dragon' being outstanding. Other notable hybrids were produced by Isabella Preston in Ottawa.

Further hybridization in the USA resulted in the Golden Clarion group with large, fragrant flowers that are rich yellow or brownish orange. Much breeding was also done in Holland, one of the most significant of the early hybrids being *L.* 'Marhan', raised towards the end of the 19th century, and still available from some specialist growers. It was used as a parent for other hybrids. In Germany in the 1930s, *L. sulphureum* (from west China and Burma) and *L. regale* were crossed to produce a range of hybrids with

trumpet-shaped flowers. The North series (e.g. 'Karen North') was developed in the latter part of the 20th century in Scotland. A notable

# Lilies in the garden

Lilies can be grown in a variety of situations. They are democratic plants, being equally at home in a small town garden or a country estate. Whatever your soil type, there is probably a lily to suit it. Lilies can be grown among shrubs or herbaceous plants in a formal or a cottage-style border, and in an informal or wild garden or woodland. Many grow well in containers. Some can also be grown for exhibition and make excellent cut flowers. The lily season normally extends from the late spring to early autumn, but commercial growers often force them to provide cut flowers or flowering pot plants all year.

## Lilies in the border

Lilies associate well with many other plants. They thrive in company since they like having their roots shaded by other plants, provided they can keep their heads in the sun. For maximum impact, plant in groups of three or five of one variety, more if space allows; too many single bulbs give a spotty effect, though this may be your only option in a tiny garden. When choosing your lilies, make sure that they tolerate your soil conditions (see Cultivation). Many of the species make good border plants,

perhaps the most outstanding being *L. regale* and the Madonna lily (*L. candidum*). Otherwise, the easiest of lilies for the border are the Asiatic hybrids. These sturdy plants, generally with upward-facing flowers, have been specially bred to thrive in a range of soils. The best of the pale colours include 'Apollo' and 'Mont Blanc' (both white), and 'Medaillon' (soft yellow). For stronger colours try 'Brushmarks' (orange marked with deep red), 'Connecticut King' (rich yellow) and 'Pirate' (red).

Trumpet lilies begin to flower from mid-summer onwards. Lilies sold under the name of Pink Perfection have flowers in a range of rich pinks that can be as dark as beetroot. They are also scented, and combine well with the grey foliage of artemisias or *Brachyglottis*. Some other outstanding members of this group include 'African Queen' (apricot) and 'Royal Gold' (rich yellow).

The Oriental hybrids dominate from late summer, but they do not tolerate lime. Outstanding members of this group include 'Casa Blanca' (white), 'Journey's End' (deep pink with maroon spots) and 'Trance' (pink with pale spots), but

■ RIGHT
Orange turkscap
lilies rise above
penstemons and
astrantias and
add height to
this border
arrangement.

■ BELOW RIGHT
Lilies with
hanging flowers
have a quiet
charm.

the real star is 'Black Beauty', a
hybrid derived from *L. speciosum* var.
*rubrum* and *L. henryi*, which can
produce over 50 blackish-red
turkscap flowers per stem.

Later-flowering lilies are more
exacting in their requirements, but
are worth persevering with. *L.
speciosum* and its forms need moist,
acid soil. *L. auratum*, the golden-
rayed lily of Japan, is perhaps the
most spectacular of all lilies, with
huge, heavily scented, glistening
white flowers banded with gold.
Small wonder that it was Monet's

## LILIES PRIZED FOR THEIR SCENT

| | |
|---|---|
| 'African Queen' | *L. lancifolium* and forms |
| *L. auratum* and forms | 'Limelight' |
| 'Black Beauty' | *L. longiflorum* (frost-free gardens only) |
| 'Black Dragon' | |
| *L. candidum* | *L. monadelphum* |
| 'Casa Blanca' | *L. nanum* |
| *L. cernuum* | Olympic group |
| *L. concolor* | Pink Perfection group |
| *L. formosanum* | *L. pumilum* |
| Golden Splendor group | *L. regale* and forms |
| 'Green Dragon' | *L. speciosum* and forms |
| *L. hansonii* | *L.* x *testaceum* |
| 'Imperial Gold' | *L. wallichianum* |
| 'Imperial Silver' | |

Asiatic hybrids with *Ligularia przewalskii* make a striking visual combination.

favourite flower. Unfortunately, it is susceptible to disease and dislikes lime, and is something of a connoisseur's plant.

Let your lilies flower above a sea of herbaceous plants such as hardy geraniums, lady's mantle (*Alchemilla mollis*) and phlox, or annuals such as love-in-a-mist (*Nigella*) and candy-tuft (*Iberis*), all gently coloured. So exotic-looking are some lilies, however, that they are best kept away from other flowering plants and enjoyed on their own against complementary foliage.

Pale-coloured lilies gleam against the pewter leaves of *Hosta* 'Blue Moon' and 'Blue Angel', or silvery lavender and achilleas. Red, yellow and orange lilies are all the more striking against a dark green yew (*Taxus*), camellia, or the rich purple leaves of *Cotinus coggygria* 'Royal Purple' or *Pittosporum*

*tenuifolium* 'Purpureum'. Ornamental grasses also make an excellent foil, as do ferns in a cool, shady area. The feathery quality of many of the latter complements the sculpted lines of the lilies.

Lilies also associate well with roses, covering the same colour range. If the lilies are scentless, plant them with scented roses such as 'Margaret Merril' (white), 'Elizabeth Harkness' (pink), 'Korresia' (yellow) or 'Fragrant Cloud' (red). Alternatively, give unscented roses a lift by combining them with fragrant lilies such as *L. regale*, 'Imperial Gold' or one of the Olympic hybrids. The Madonna lily (*L. candidum*) is a traditional cottage-garden plant that blends happily with old-fashioned roses such as 'Buff Beauty' (apricot) or the much loved, striped *R. gallica* 'Versicolor' (pink and crimson).

In a white garden try 'Casa Blanca', *L. auratum*, *L. candidum*, 'Green Magic', 'Imperial Silver', 'Mont Blanc', *L. regale* or *L. wallichianum* with 'Iceberg' roses and *Gypsophila paniculata* 'Bristol Fairy'. *Penstemon* 'White Bedder', *Anaphalis triplinervis* (grey-green leaves) and *Hebe rakaiensis* fill out the arrangement, with the grey-green leaflets of *Melianthus major* in the background, and the indispensable grey-green lambs' ears (*Stachys byzantina*) to the fore. A pastel scheme in a garden can include one of the lilies from the Pink Perfection group or the

Spiky *eryngiums* provide a subtle contrast to these elegant lilies.

■ BELOW
**Many lilies can be grown in light shade between trees and shrubs.**

popular 'Côte d'Azur' with achilleas and blue *Campanula latifolia*. For a golden scheme, try planting varieties from the Golden Splendor group with the Welsh poppy *Meconopsis cambrica* and golden-leaved shrubs such as *Philadelphus coronarius* 'Aureus' or *Choisya ternata* 'Sundance'. You could turn the temperature right up with a rich orange scheme that includes *L. henryi* with *Crocosmia* 'Lucifer' (scarlet) and *Lobelia* 'Dark Crusader' (blood red) against the rich purple of *Cotinus coggygria* 'Royal Purple'.

Some excellent lilies to try for a beautifully scented garden include *L. regale, L. candidum, L. speciosum* and *L. auratum*. Most Trumpet and Oriental lilies are also scented, some very heavily so. Companion plants could include *Rosa* 'Margaret Merril', annual tobacco plants (*Nicotiana*), the daylily *Hemerocallis citrina, Iris graminea* (with flowers that smell of stewed plums), herbs such as thyme, lavender and rosemary, and old-fashioned pinks (*Dianthus*). Back these with honeysuckle (*Lonicera*), and a mock orange such as *Philadelphus* 'Manteau d'Hermine' or a buddleia.

## Lilies in woodland and wild gardens

Some lily species flourish in light shade. *L. pyrenaicum, L. martagon* and the American species and their hybrids can be grown beneath deciduous trees, provided the leaf canopy is not too dense. *L. martagon* is a variable plant, and it is a good idea to mix its different forms that range in colour from white through shades of dusky pink to a deep rosy purple. The Bellingham hybrids

### LILIES SUITABLE FOR LIGHT WOODLAND

| |
|---|
| Bellingham hybrids |
| *L. hansonii* |
| *L. henryi* |
| *L. lancifolium* |
| *L.* 'Marhan' |
| *L. martagon* and forms |
| *L. monadelphum* |
| *L. pardalinum* |
| *L. pyrenaicum* |
| *L. regale* |

■ LEFT

Some hybrid lilies that are close to woodland species thrive under a light canopy of trees.

readily by stem bulbils (see Propagation and hybridizing). In frost-free gardens, the Easter lily (*L. longiflorum*) is a prime candidate for massed planting.

## Lilies in containers

Lilies thrive in containers, and will give pleasure over a number of years, given attention. They are invaluable

offer similar possibilities in a different colour range, from yellow to orange and red. They increase rapidly. As companions, choose plants that enjoy the same conditions. In cool, acid soil, you could have great success teaming *L. monadelphum* with the beautiful Himalayan blue poppy (*Meconopsis betonicifolia*). Under trees, interplant with periwinkle (*Vinca*), ferns or *Cyclamen hederifolium*, which would flower after the lilies have died down. Hellebores would provide spring interest and their evergreen foliage would help shade the lilies' roots.

In a more open situation, a sunny bank of *L. regale* en masse would be an impressive sight. Where the soil does not dry out, try the much loved tiger lily (*L. lancifolium*), with orange-red flowers, which increases

■ LEFT
'Star Gazer' is one of the best lilies for growing in containers.

■ BELOW
Place pots of *L. regale* near seats to enjoy
the fragrance to the full.

for the patio, balcony or roof garden. Town dwellers who work during the day will particularly appreciate those that release their scent at dusk to attract pollinating moths.

Asiatic, Trumpet and Oriental lilies all thrive in pots, as do many of the species. *L. regale* is especially recommended. 'Mont Blanc' (white) and 'Harmony' (salmon-orange) are sturdy, short-stemmed varieties, but there are other modern hybrids that have been specially bred for containers. They include dwarf Orientals, of which the best is probably 'Star Gazer' (rich reddish-pink with darker spots). Dwarf Asiatics (Pixie lilies) include varieties with crimson, orange and buff-coloured flowers. They grow to about 30cm (12in) and are suitable for growing in window boxes and with trailing ivies, *Campanula carpatica* and other low-growing plants.

Other dwarf lilies include the Aladdin series, bred from *L. longiflorum* and Asiatic hybrids, that are no higher than 90cm (3ft) tall. Three lilies known collectively as Little Rascals ('Mr Sam', 'Mr Rudd' and 'Mr Ed') grow no larger than 45cm (18in).

Pots of lilies can be moved around at will and brought centre-stage when in flower. By carefully choosing your varieties, you can have lilies in flower through the summer, into early autumn. Growing them in containers also gives you the opportunity to grow those species that dislike your garden's soil. Pot-grown lilies also allow you to indulge in a little horticultural hoodwinking. Drop them into the border to fill any gaps that open up as the season advances. To reduce the need for watering and to keep the roots cool, dig a hole and sink the pots into the ground rather than standing them on the soil surface.

# Botany and classification

Lilies are bulbous perennials. The bulbs are composed of fleshy, overlapping scales, which are actually modified leaves that act as an energy store. Some are no larger than marbles, while others are closer to artichokes. Generally, the scales are arranged around a single growing point, and have a round basal plate. The North American *L. pardalinum*, however, is rhizomatous and develops a broad, basal plate with several growing points.

In spring, a single, unbranched stem emerges from each bulb. After flowering, usually in mid- to late summer, seed is produced and the stem withers and dies back, usually to below ground level, though *L. candidum* and a few other species have a rosette of overwintering basal leaves. This is when most bulbs experience an increase in rooting activity. Thick, fleshy roots delve deep into the soil, pulling the bulb downwards. Fibrous roots emerging from around the basal plate also now develop. In many cases the portion of stem below ground level also produces roots. The lily is still active, therefore, even though no signs of growth are visible above ground level. Most lilies have strong, upright stems, but a few of the smaller species have thin, wiry ones. The leaves are generally strap- to spear-shaped, and can either be scattered up the stem (in some cases clasping the stem), or arranged alternately or in whorls.

The number of flowers produced by a single bulb varies and can depend on cultural conditions. They can be carried singly, or in racemes of up to 50 or more. Most are carried on a single stalk, but in some cases the stalk divides and carries two or three flowers. In the case of many Asiatic species, the flower stalks are progressively shorter towards the stem tip, so that the overall effect is of a flowering pyramid.

Lily flowers are composed of six overlapping "tepals" (petal-like structures but distinct from petals and sepals). They can be bowl-, trumpet- or funnel-shaped, or

■ BELOW
Some lily flowers are heavily spotted with a darker colour.

■ ABOVE
Lily bulbs are made up of fleshy, overlapping scales.

■ BELOW
Lily leaves are elliptic to lance-shaped
and vary in length.

turkscap (usually pendent, with
sharply reflexed tepals). Some bowl-
shaped flowers open virtually flat
and are star-like. They can be of
uniform colour, but are sometimes
flushed with a second colour
towards the base; in some cases, the
flushing is restricted to the outside
of the tepal. The inside of the tepal
can be spotted, sometimes heavily
so, or have a central coloured band.
It is assumed that these markings
guide pollinating insects towards
the centre of the flower. Some lily
flowers (notably *L. speciosum* and *L.
auratum*) have papillae, which are
small, soft, pointed protuberances
at the base of the tepal.

The flower colours range from
white, through all shades of pink to
deep red, yellow and orange; there
is no blue or purple. Spots can be
either a darker shade of the main
colour, maroon, brown, green or
purple-black. In all cases the
stamens are prominent, often
bearing conspicuous red or yellow
pollen that is itself a decorative,
distinctive feature.

Many lilies are also highly
fragrant, while a few species have
a distinctly unpleasant smell.
Others, ones with red flowers in
particular, have no scent at all.

■ LEFT
A lily flower with
coloured bands and
conspicuous papillae.

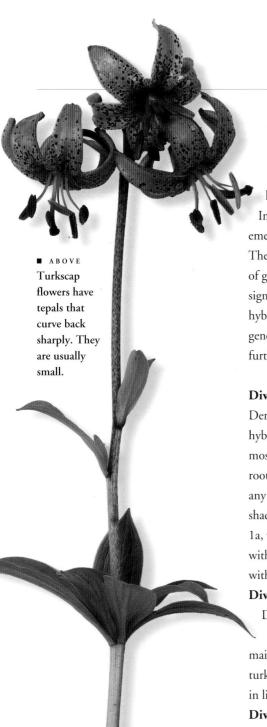

■ ABOVE
Turkscap
flowers have
tepals that
curve back
sharply. They
are usually
small.

■ BELOW
A lily with outward-facing, trumpet-shaped flowers.

## Lily divisions

Owing to the accessibility of their reproductive parts, lilies lend themselves to hybridization. Interbreeding has resulted in the emergence of distinct, hybrid groups. The divisions are for the convenience of gardeners, and have small botanical significance. With continued hybridization and the advent of genetic engineering, it is likely that further divisions will be created.

**Division 1 (Asiatic Hybrids)**
Derived from Asiatic species and hybrids, these are sturdy, hardy, mostly unscented, usually stem-rooting lilies suitable for growing in any well-drained soil in sun or partial shade. There are three subdivisions: 1a, with upward-facing flowers; 1b, with outward-facing flowers; and 1c, with pendent flowers.

**Division 2 (Martagon Hybrids)**
Derived mainly from *L. martagon* and *L. hansonii*, these are hardy, mainly stem-rooting lilies with turkscap flowers, suitable for growing in light shade or woodland.

**Division 3 (Candidum Hybrids)**
Derived from *L. candidum, L. chalcedonicum* and other European species, excluding *L. martagon*, these comprise a small group of lilies with sometimes scented, turkscap flowers. They are not usually stem-rooting and will grow in full sun or partial shade.

**Division 4 (American Hybrids)**
Derived from American species, these lilies can be rhizomatous, with sometimes scented, usually turkscap flowers. Most are not stem-rooting and will grow in any well-drained soil in sun or partial shade.

**Division 5 (Longiflorum Hybrids)**
Derived from *L. formosanum* and *L. longiflorum*, these comprise a small but growing group of lilies with fragrant, trumpet- or funnel-shaped flowers, usually grown for the cut

■ BELOW
An Asiatic hybrid with bowl-shaped
flowers opening from upward-facing buds.

flower market. Crosses with Asiatic
hybrids have produced sturdier
plants more suitable for general
garden use.

## Division 6 (Trumpet and Aurelian Hybrids)

Derived from Asiatic species, other
than *L. auratum, L. japonicum, L.
rubellum* and *L. speciosum*, these are
mostly hardy, fragrant, stem-rooting
lilies for fertile, well-drained soil,
preferably in partial shade. There are
four subdivisions: 6a, with trumpet-
shaped flowers; 6b, with usually
outward-facing, bowl-shaped flowers;
6c, with shallow, bowl-shaped flowers
that often open flat; 6d, with tepals
that are distinctly recurved.

## Division 7 (Oriental Hybrids)

Derived from *L. auratum, L.
japonicum, L. rubellum* and *L.
speciosum*, these are late-flowering
lilies, often with scented flowers.
Most are lime-hating and need sun or
partial shade. There are four
subdivisions: 7a, with trumpet-
shaped flowers; 7b, with bowl-shaped
flowers; 7c, with flat flowers; 7d, with
tepals that are distinctly recurved.

## Division 8

Consists of all hybrids that do not fit
into the other groups.

## Division 9

All species lilies and their forms.

# Plant Catalogue

In the following catalogue,
lilies are listed alphabetically in
two sections: species, and their
forms and cultivars; and
hybrids. Since each bulb has
only a single growing point,
only the height is given, not its
spread. Note that heights will
vary in cultivation depending
on the climate, season and soil
type; species in particular are
likely to show extreme
variation. The dimension cited
is the maximum each lily
can be expected to achieve.

Individual cultivation
requirements are given for all
species, since these can vary
widely; for the garden use of
hybrids, see Botany and
classification.

# Species lilies

■ ABOVE RIGHT
*L. AURATUM* (GOLDEN-
RAYED LILY)

Species lily from Japan (Division 9). In late
summer to autumn, it produces large, bowl-
shaped, heavily scented flowers; the tepals are
white, usually spotted with crimson, with
conspicuous yellow bands and fleshy papillae.
Height to 1.5m (5ft). *L. auratum* has the
largest flowers of any lily; it prefers lime-
free soil and can be difficult to establish.

■ RIGHT
*L. CANADENSE* (MEADOW
LILY, WILD MEADOW LILY)

Species lily from eastern North America
(Division 9). In summer, bell-shaped,
slightly scented flowers hang from graceful
stems; the tepals are yellow, spotted with
maroon at the base. Height to 1.5m (5ft).
*L. canadense* succeeds best in lime-free,
leafy soil in partial shade.

■ RIGHT

## *L. CANDIDUM* (MADONNA LILY)

Species lily from the Balkans and the eastern Mediterranean (Division 9). In summer, erect stems carry trumpet-shaped, fragrant flowers; the tepals are white with yellow inside at the base. Height to 2m (6ft). *L. candidum* needs neutral to alkaline soil; plant the bulbs shallowly in early autumn.

■ BELOW RIGHT

## *L. DUCHARTREI* (MARBLE MARTAGON LILY)

Species lily from western China (Division 9). In summer, it produces fragrant, turkscap flowers; the tepals are white, heavily spotted and veined with reddish-purple. Height to 1m (40in). *L. duchartrei* tolerates lime, but is best in leafy, well-drained soil in a cool, lightly shaded position; it spreads by stolons and will rapidly form colonies in good conditions.

■ ABOVE RIGHT

*L. FORMOSANUM*

Species lily from Taiwan (Division 9). In
late summer and early autumn, large,
fragrant, trumpet-shaped flowers open
from buds that are strongly flushed with
wine-purple (see inset); the tepals are pure
white inside. Height to 1.5m (5ft).
*L. formosanum* is an elegant plant. It
needs moist, acid soil and, in cold districts,
protection from frost; the variant var.
*pricei* is hardier and much smaller.

■ RIGHT

*L. HENRYI*

Clump-forming species lily from central
China (Division 9). In late summer,
elegant stems carry hanging, lightly
scented, turkscap flowers; the tepals are
bright orange with darker spots. Height
to 3m (10ft). Best in neutral to alkaline
soil in light shade, *L. henryi* is an easy
species to grow.

■ LEFT
### *L. LEICHTLINII* VAR. *MAXIMOWICZII*

Species lily from Japan and central Korea, a variant of the rarer *L. leichtlinii* (see inset). In summer, it produces hanging, unscented, turkscap flowers; the tepals are bright orange-red, spotted with purple-brown (the straight species has lemon-yellow tepals spotted with maroon). Height to 2m (6ft). *L. leichtlinii* var. *maximowiczii* is an easily grown lily that is best in lime-free soil in sun or light shade; it is readily increased from seed.

■ ABOVE

*L. LONGIFLORUM* (EASTER LILY, BERMUDA LILY)

Species lily from southern Japan and Taiwan (Division 9). In summer, large, fragrant, trumpet-shaped flowers open from pale buds; the tepals are pure white. Height to 1m (40in). *L. longiflorum* is easy to grow and tolerates lime, but will not withstand many degrees of frost; it is grown commercially for the cut flower trade.

■ RIGHT

### *L. MARTAGON* (TURKSCAP LILY, MARTAGON LILY)

Species lily that occurs in a range from north-west Europe to north-west Asia (Division 9). In early to mid-summer, slightly unpleasantly scented, turkscap flowers hang from the stems; the tepals are dull pink, spotted with maroon. Height to 2m (6ft). Naturally occurring variants include var. *album*, with white flowers (see inset), and var. *cattaniae*, with maroon flowers. *L. martagon* and its forms are useful for naturalizing in almost any well-drained soil in sun or light shade.

■ LEFT

### *L. NEPALENSE*

Rhizomatous species lily from northern India, Nepal and Bhutan (Division 9). In early to mid-summer, erect or arching stems carry funnel-shaped, sometimes unpleasantly scented flowers; the tepals are greenish-yellow, stained with purple on the inside. Height to 1m (40in). *L. nepalense* needs acid soil in partial shade; the underground stems grow horizontally and may emerge some distance from where the bulb was planted.

■ ABOVE
### *L. PARDALINUM*
### (LEOPARD LILY)

Rhizomatous species lily from the western USA (Division 9). In summer, unscented turkscap flowers hang from the stems; the tepals are bright orange-red, darker red at the tips, and with dark brown spots (sometimes margined yellow) towards the base. Height to 2.4m (8ft). Given damp, humus-rich soil, in sun or light shade, *L. pardalinum* is an easy species to grow.

■ LEFT
### *L. PYRENAICUM*

Clump-forming species lily from the Pyrenees (Division 9). In early to mid-summer, unpleasant-smelling turkscap flowers hang from the stems; the tepals are greenish-yellow, spotted and lined with black towards the base. Height to 90cm (3ft). *L. pyrenaicum* needs neutral to alkaline soil in sun or light shade and is easy to grow.

■ ABOVE

*L. REGALE* (REGAL LILY)

Species lily from western China (Division 9). In mid-summer, it produces sweetly fragrant, trumpet-shaped flowers; the tepals are white, yellow at the base, stained purple outside. Height to 2m (6ft). *L. regale* is the easiest of all species for the garden, and tolerates most well-drained soils. Seed-raised plants flower within three years of sowing. Naturally occurring variants include var. *album*, with pure white flowers.

■ RIGHT

*L. SPECIOSUM* VAR. *ALBUM*

Species lily from eastern China, Japan and Taiwan (Division 9). In late summer and early autumn, erect stems carry large, fragrant, outward-facing or hanging, turkscap flowers; the tepals are white, with prominent papillae. Height to 2m (6ft). *L. speciosum* var. *album* is an outstanding lily for the border; it needs moist, acid soil and prefers partial shade.

■ LEFT

### L. SPECIOSUM 'UCHIDA'

Lily of garden origin, a selection of a species from eastern China, Japan and Taiwan (Division 9). In late summer and early autumn, erect stems carry large, fragrant, outward-facing or hanging, turkscap flowers; the tepals are brilliant crimson, spotted with green or darker red, with white tips. Height to 2m (6ft). *L. speciosum* 'Uchida' is one of several outstanding selections; others include 'Grand Commander' (lilac-purple tepals, spotted red) and 'Krätzeri' (white tepals, striped green on the reverse).

■ RIGHT

### L. TSINGTAUENSE

Species lily from eastern China and Korea (Division 9). In mid-summer, it produces upward-facing, unscented, bowl-shaped flowers that open flat; the tepals are orange or vermilion-orange, spotted with purple. Height to 90cm (3ft). Distinctive and elegant, *L. tsingtauense* thrives in moist, acid soil in full sun or partial shade; it tolerates some lime.

# Hybrid lilies

■ RIGHT
'ACAPULCO'

Oriental hybrid lily (Division 7d). In mid-summer, it produces large flowers with recurving, fragrant, deep pink tepals. Height to 90cm (3ft). 'Acapulco' is valued by flower arrangers for its intense colour.

■ BELOW
'ADMIRATION'

Asiatic hybrid lily (Division 1a). In early to mid-summer, it produces large, upward-facing, scentless flowers; the tepals are creamy yellow. Height to 40cm (16in). 'Admiration' is excellent in containers.

■ ABOVE
AFRICAN QUEEN GROUP

Aurelian hybrid lilies (Division 6a). In mid- and late summer, erect stems carry large, outward-facing, trumpet-shaped, richly fragrant flowers; the tepals are deep tangerine-apricot, veined with dark purple outside. Height to 2m (6ft). The group designation indicates that plants sold under this name may vary in intensity of flower colour, but all make outstanding border plants.

■ LEFT
BELLINGHAM HYBRIDS

American hybrid lilies (Division 4). In early and mid-summer, they produce medium-sized, occasionally slightly fragrant, turkscap flowers; the tepals vary in colour from yellow to orange and orange-red, all spotted deep brown. Height to 1.5m (5ft). The Bellingham hybrids are good for naturalizing in light dappled shade; they require acid soil.

■ ABOVE
'BELLE EPOQUE'

Oriental hybrid lily (Division 7b). From mid-summer to early autumn, it produces large, outward-facing, bowl-shaped, scented flowers, up to eight per stem; the tepals vary in colour from white to soft pink, with a central cream band. Height to 1m (40in). 'Belle Epoque' benefits from regular feeding.

■ RIGHT
### 'BRONWEN NORTH'

Asiatic hybrid lily (Division 1c). In early summer, medium-sized, slightly scented, turkscap flowers hang from the stems; the tepals are pale mauve-pink, spotted and lined with purple. 'Bronwen North' is a striking, easily grown lily for the mixed border.

■ BELOW
### 'CASA BLANCA'

Oriental hybrid lily (Division 7b). In mid- to late summer, stiff stems carry heavily scented, bowl-shaped flowers; the tepals are pure white. Height to 1.2m (4ft). A prolific lily, 'Casa Blanca' is of value both in the garden and as a cut flower.

■ LEFT
**'CENTURION'**

Hybrid lily (Division 5). In mid-summer, it produces large, outward-facing, sweetly scented, funnel- to trumpet-shaped flowers, up to four per stem, that open flat; the tepals are creamy salmon, with heavy spotting towards the base. Height to 90cm (3ft). 'Centurion' is excellent as a cut flower.

■ RIGHT
**'CONCORDE'**

Asiatic hybrid lily (Division 1a). From early to mid-summer, sturdy stems carry large, upward-facing, unscented, bowl-shaped flowers; the tepals are lemon-yellow, greenish at the base, speckled chocolate-red. Height to 1m (40in). 'Concorde' is an excellent lily for the mixed or herbaceous border.

■ RIGHT
'CONNECTICUT KING'

Asiatic hybrid lily (Division 1a). In early
summer, unscented, star-shaped flowers
appear; the tepals are rich deep yellow,
slightly paler at the base. Height to 1m
(40in). A strong grower, 'Connecticut King'
is the most popular yellow hybrid lily.

■ BELOW
'COTE D'AZUR'

Asiatic hybrid lily (Division 1a). In early to
mid-summer, strong stems carry
unscented, bowl-shaped flowers; the tepals
are deep pink, paler pink towards the base,
and are lightly spotted. Height to 1m
(40in). 'Côte d'Azur' is a sturdy lily that
is ideal for containers or the border.

■ LEFT
### 'DONAU'

Hybrid lily (Division 8). In mid-summer, it produces large, upward-facing, sweetly scented, bowl-shaped flowers, up to four per stem; the tepals are soft salmon-orange. Height to 1m (40in). 'Donau' is a good lily for flower arranging.

■ BELOW
### 'GRAN SASSO'

Asiatic hybrid lily (Division 1a). In early and mid-summer, it produces large, upward-facing, unscented flowers, up to six per stem; the tepals are rich orange, heavily spotted with maroon. Height to 1m (40in). 'Gran Sasso' is an excellent variety for general garden use.

■ RIGHT
### 'EROS'

Asiatic hybrid lily (Division 1c). In mid-summer, it produces nodding, fragrant, turkscap flowers; the tepals are pinkish-orange, spotted maroon. Height to 1.2m (4ft). 'Eros' is an easily grown lily that associates well with cottage-garden plants.

■ ABOVE

### 'HER GRACE'

Asiatic hybrid lily (Division 1a). In mid-summer, it produces large, upward-facing, unscented, bowl-shaped flowers; the tepals are rich clear yellow. Height to 1.2m (4ft). 'Her Grace' is excellent for general garden use, in a container and as a cut flower.

■ RIGHT

### 'KAREN NORTH'

Asiatic hybrid lily (Division 1c). In mid-summer, it produces medium-sized, lightly scented, turkscap flowers; the tepals are orange-pink, lightly spotted with darker pink. Height to 1.4m (4½ft). 'Karen North' is an elegant, prolific lily.

■ LEFT
'LITTLE JOY'

Oriental hybrid lily (Division 7d). In early summer, sturdy stems carry unscented, recurved flowers; the tepals are pink to soft red, spotted with dark maroon. Height to 35cm (14in). A Little Rascal type, 'Little Joy' is an outstanding lily for containers and window boxes.

■ RIGHT
'MONEYMAKER'

Hybrid lily (Division 8). In mid-summer, it produces large, outward-facing, sweetly scented, funnel- to trumpet-shaped flowers, up to six per stem, that open flat; the tepals are clear pink, with light spotting towards the base. Height to 1m (40in). 'Moneymaker' is excellent as a cut flower.

■ ABOVE

'MONT BLANC'

Asiatic hybrid lily (Division 1a). In early to
mid-summer, stout stems carry scentless,
bowl-shaped flowers; the tepals are white,
sparsely spotted with brown towards the
base. Height to 70cm (28in). 'Mont Blanc'
is a vigorous lily, suitable for the border
and for cutting.

■ RIGHT

'MRS R.O. BACKHOUSE'

Martagon hybrid lily (Division 2). In early
to mid-summer, unscented turkscap
flowers hang from the stems; the tepals
are orange-yellow with light spotting and
are flushed pink on the outside. Height
to 1.3m (52in). 'Mrs R.O. Backhouse'
is one of the oldest hybrids still in
general cultivation.

■ LEFT
**'ORANGE PIXIE'**

Oriental hybrid lily
(Division 1a). In
summer, medium-sized,
upward-facing,
scentless, bowl-shaped
flowers appear; the
pointed tepals are
bright orange-red, with
chocolate-maroon spots.
Height to 40cm (16in).
'Orange Pixie' is an
excellent lily for a
container; the flowers
are large in relation to
the size of the plant.

■ ABOVE
**'PEGGY NORTH'**

Asiatic hybrid lily (Division 1c). In
mid-summer, it produces medium-sized,
lightly scented, turkscap flowers; the
tepals are glowing orange, spotted with
dark brown. Height to 1.5m (5ft). 'Peggy
North' is an excellent lily for a mixed or
herbaceous border.

■ LEFT
**'ROMA'**

Asiatic hybrid lily
(Division 1a). In early
to mid-summer, strong
stems carry upward-
facing, scented, bowl-
shaped flowers; the
wide tepals are creamy
white, lightly spotted
with maroon towards
the base. Height to
1.2m (4ft). 'Roma'
has dark foliage that
contrasts well with
the flowers.

■ RIGHT
'ROYAL CLASS'

Oriental hybrid lily
(Division 7b). From
mid-summer to early
autumn, it produces
large, outward-facing,
bowl-shaped, scented
flowers, up to seven per
stem; the tepals vary in
colour from white to
soft pink, with a central
yellow band and
prominent papillae.
Height to 90cm (3ft).
'Royal Class' benefits
from regular feeding.

■ LEFT
'SANTA
BARBARA'

Oriental hybrid
lily (Division 7b).
From mid-
summer to early
autumn, it
produces medium-
sized, outward-
facing, bowl-
shaped, scented
flowers, up to
eight per stem; the
tepals are soft
pink, with pink
papillae. Height to
35cm (14in).
'Santa Barbara' is
excellent for
containers.

■ RIGHT
'SCIENCE
FICTION'

Hybrid lily
(Division 8). In
mid-summer, large,
outward-facing,
trumpet- to funnel-
shaped, unscented
flowers, up to six
per stem, open from
slightly hairy buds;
the tepals are
maroon-red, with
light spotting
towards the base.
Height to 1m
(40in). 'Science
Fiction' is excellent
as a cut flower.

■ ABOVE
'SHUKSAN'

American hybrid lily (Division 4), a
selection of the Bellingham hybrids. In
mid-summer, sturdy stems carry lightly
scented, turkscap flowers; the tepals are
tangerine-yellow, heavily spotted with
black or reddish-brown, and have red tips.
Height to 1.2m (4ft). In good conditions –
acid soil in partial shade –'Shuksan'
increases rapidly.

■ LEFT
'SILHOUETTE'

Asiatic hybrid lily
(Division 1a). In
summer, it
produces large,
upward-facing,
scentless flowers;
the tepals are
white, flushed
creamy yellow at
the base, and
spotted and edged
maroon. Height
to 1m (40in). The
unique markings
of 'Silhouette' are
best appreciated
in flower
arrangements.

■ LEFT
## 'STAR GAZER'

Oriental hybrid lily (Division 7c). From mid-summer, it produces large, outward-facing, bowl-shaped, unscented flowers that open flat; the tepals are rich crimson-pink with darker spots. Height to 1.5m (5ft). A vigorous lily, 'Star Gazer' is excellent both in the garden and in a container; it needs acid soil.

■ RIGHT
## 'WHITE HENRYI'

Aurelian hybrid lily (Division 6c). In mid-summer, it produces large, fragrant, outward-facing flowers that open flat; the tepals are white, flushed deep orange at the base and with rust-red papillae. Height to 1.5m (5ft). 'White Henryi' is a vigorous, disease-resistant lily.

# Buying lilies

Lilies are available as dormant bulbs, usually in the autumn and spring. The majority are imported from the Netherlands. It is best to buy in the autumn, as soon as possible after the bulbs have been lifted. Bulbs bought in the spring may have dried out excessively, and can fail to establish unless they have been stored in appropriate conditions over winter.

Popular species and varieties are sold in garden centres, loose or pre-packed in small quantities, usually in straw. Packs of mixed lilies are cheap, but they can be disappointing if the bulbs flower at different times or grow to different heights. For rarer lilies contact bulb suppliers, most of whom supply by mail order (large orders are usually discounted). In the case of rare species, only seed may be available, either from a specialist seed supplier or a lily society. When buying, try to

■ BELOW
*L. wilsonii* is a rare lily from Japan. It is usually available only as seed from specialist lily growers or seed suppliers.

■ BELOW
**Lily bulbs are usually packed in straw or some other dry material.**

obtain guaranteed disease-free bulbs, even though they are more expensive than uncertified stock. Bulbs affected by virus will probably fail to thrive and die out after a few years, and will also introduce the virus into your soil, which may affect other plants. Also check that you are buying large, plump, healthy bulbs. Avoid any that look dried out or withered, or that show signs of fungal growth.

Lilies are also available in containers in full growth, sometimes when in flower. They are often sold as flowering pot plants by florists and in supermarkets, intended for enjoyment indoors. After flowering they can be placed outside, and the bulbs planted in the open garden once the top-growth has died down.

■ ABOVE
**Lilies are sometimes sold in full growth in containers.**

# Cultivation

All lilies need free-draining soil, preferably with some shade at the base of the stem. They will not grow in heavy, waterlogged clay. Most are best in full sun, but some need protection from the hot summer sun. No lily will thrive in dense shade but a number are adapted to light woodland, and these can be grown among deciduous trees and shrubs provided the leaf canopy is not too dense at flowering time. The best way of ensuring that the roots stay cool is to grow the lilies among low-growing shrubs such as dwarf rhododendrons (if your soil is acid), or perennials. Excessive damp at the roots can be fatal. Shelter from strong winds is also desirable, particularly for tall varieties.

Soil fertility is equally important. Try to improve the soil before planting by digging in leaf mould (dry leaves that have been stored and allowed to break down for at least two years), particularly for woodland species, or well-rotted organic matter

| LILIES THAT TOLERATE A RANGE OF SOIL TYPES | |
| --- | --- |
| L. amabile | L. lancifolium and forms |
| Asiatic hybrids | L. maculatum |
| L. bulbiferum var. croceum | L. 'Marhan' |
| L. cernuum | L. martagon |
| L. chalcedonicum | L. monadelphum |
| L. x dalhansonii | L. pomponium |
| L. davidii and forms | L. pyrenaicum and forms |
| L. hansonii | L. regale |
| L. henryi | L. x testaceum |

## TESTING YOUR SOIL WITH A SOIL-TESTING KIT

1 Take a small sample of your garden soil from 5–7.5cm (2–3in) below the surface for the most representative reading.

2 Allow the sample to dry out slowly, then place it in the test tube and add water as recommended by the manufacturer.

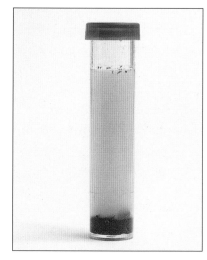

3 Shake the test tube and wait for the contents to settle. The colour indicates the acidity of your soil, and should be compared with the chart supplied.

## LILIES THAT TOLERATE ALKALINE SOIL

*(* indicates prefers neutral to alkaline conditions)*

L. amabile

Asiatic hybrids

L. brownii

L. bulbiferum var. croceum

L. candidum*

L. chalcedonicum

L. x dalhansonii

L. davidii and forms

L. hansonii

L. henryi*

L. lancifolium

L. leucanthum var. centifolium

L. monadelphum

L. pomponium*

L. pumilum

L. pyrenaicum and forms*

L. regale

L. sargentii

L. x testaceum

Trumpet and Aurelian hybrids

(either farmyard manure or garden compost). Cultivating the soil also improves moisture-retention on light, free-draining ground, and opens up the texture of clay soils. The latter can be further improved by forking in plenty of grit.

Most lilies prefer acid to neutral soil. Some tolerate lime, while a few prefer it. However, many modern hybrids have been bred to thrive in a range of soil types. If you do not know whether your soil is acid or alkaline, test it with a chemical soil-testing kit or an electronic meter, or restrict your choice to lilies that will grow in either. Since conditions may vary from one part of your garden to another, test various sites. You can adjust the pH of your soil to suit a particular lily. To raise the alkalinity add lime, and to change the acidity use flowers of sulphur. However, it is better to choose lilies that thrive in the current conditions rather than modifying the soil to suit the lilies. Alternatively, grow them in containers.

■ ABOVE

**Many modern hybrid lilies tolerate a range of soil types.**

## LILIES THAT REQUIRE ACID SOIL

L. auratum and forms

L. lancifolium

L. leichtlinii

L. nepalense

Oriental hybrids

L. rubellum

L. speciosum

L. wallichianum

# Planting

Lily bulbs should be planted immediately after purchase, but if you must delay because of unsuitable weather, store them in a cool, dark, frost-free place. Mist them occasionally with a fungicide to prevent them from drying out, and to keep them free of fungal growths.

Lilies establish most quickly if planted promptly when their annual growth cycle has finished. This is particularly beneficial to stem-rooting lilies. Early planting enables the stem to build up a good root system before it emerges above ground level in the spring, making a stronger plant. However, in areas with harsh winters, delay planting until the spring. Take care when handling the bulbs, since they are easily damaged.

The planting depth depends on whether the lily produces annual roots from the stem (stem-rooting), or from the base of the bulb only (see Botany and classification). Plant the latter, basal-rooting lilies 10–15cm (4–6in) deep, and stem-rooting lilies 20–25cm (8–10in) deep. Exceptions are *L. candidum* and *L.* x *testaceum,* which should be planted so that the

**DEAD-HEADING**

Remove flowers as they fade.

**PLANTING LILIES**

**1** Unless your soil is very free-draining, fork in grit at the rate of about one bucketful per sq m (yd).

**2** Dig a planting hole about 30cm (12in) deep. Work in organic matter and a handful of bonemeal at the base of the hole.

**3** Set the bulbs in position. An odd number of the same variety looks best.

■ LEFT
**LEFT**
Lilies reward care
and attention
with a sumptuous
display.

nose of the bulb is only just covered.
Tall-growing lilies benefit from
staking. Either use a proprietary ring
stake, or individual canes. Insert the
stakes at planting time to avoid
damaging the bulbs, and tie in the
stems as they grow.

After flowering, unless you
want seed for propagation (see
Propagation and hybridizing),
remove the fading flower head. This
will help prevent viral infections
striking as the flower withers, and
also channel the bulb's energy into
building up next year's display.

**4** Backfill with the excavated soil,
incorporating more organic matter as
you do so.

**5** Fork in a little general fertilizer.

**6** Mark the position of the bulbs with
a short stake. Insert stakes for
taller varieties.

# Growing in containers

**Pots of fragrant *L. regale* scent the air on a warm summer's evening.**

Many lilies thrive in containers, and that is the best way of growing those that dislike the soil in your garden. Stem-rooting lilies tend to do better in pots than basal-rooting lilies. Dwarf lilies have been specially bred for pot culture. Most types of container are suitable. Terracotta or stone containers are porous and less likely to become waterlogged than plastic; they are also heavier, and less likely to be blown over. Wooden half-barrels can also be used, but they are less durable. Plastic containers are light and easy to move around.

The container must be deep enough to let you plant the bulbs at the correct depth (see Planting). Unless acidity is important, loam-based compost (soil mix) gives the best results, being less likely to become waterlogged or excessively dry than one based on peat or coir. For improved drainage, mix in horticultural grit at the rate of two parts compost (soil mix) to one of grit. Since most commercially prepared composts (soil mixes) are alkaline, you should use ericaceous compost (soil mix) for lilies that need acid soil.

The nutrients in proprietary composts (soil mixes) are rapidly depleted, so supplementary feeding is necessary to ensure that the lilies flower best. You can either incorporate a slow-release fertilizer on planting, or apply a high-potash fertilizer (to promote flower production) while the lilies are in active growth. Apply all fertilizers according to the manufacturer's instructions, but stop feeding once the flower buds have formed. Apply a feed immediately after flowering to build up the bulb's strength.

It is essential to keep lilies well-watered during the growing season. Failure to do this can result in blind shoots (see Pests, diseases and other

## PLANTING LILIES IN A CONTAINER

**1** Place broken crocks or stones at the base of the container for fast drainage.

**2** Cover the crocks with a layer of horticultural grit.

**3** Fill the container to the appropriate depth with compost (soil mix) mixed with grit, perlite or vermiculite.

**4** Set the bulbs in position. An odd number looks best. For tall varieties, insert stakes at this stage.

**5** Fill the container with the compost (soil mix), leaving a gap of about 2.5cm (1in) between the surface and the rim of the container to allow for watering. Add pellets of slow-release fertilizer as recommended by the manufacturer.

**6** Water well, and top-dress with grit, to prevent excessive evaporation from the compost (soil mix) surface and to deter slugs. Water regularly when the bulbs are in active growth.

problems). Remove the flowers as they fade, unless you wish to gather seed.

In winter, protect them from freezing weather. Either wrap the container loosely in hessian (burlap) or a permeable material, or take it into a porch or unheated greenhouse. In early spring, before new growth has emerged, tilt the container and

scrape away the top 2.5cm (1in) of compost (soil mix). Replace it with fresh compost (soil mix), and then top-dress with grit.

Repot the bulbs every two or three years. When the lilies have died down in the autumn, tilt the container on its side and scrape out the compost (soil mix). Handle the bulbs with

care; if they are stem-rooting, there will probably be some stem present, which is easily damaged. Discard any old, withered bulbs. Wash out the container, and replant in fresh compost (soil mix). Any bulblets or offsets can be potted up and grown on until they reach flowering size (see Propagation and hybridizing).

# Propagation and hybridizing

You can increase your stock of lilies by a variety of techniques. All species can be raised from seed, an easy method that ensures virus-free stock. Hybrids and named varieties can only be increased vegetatively. It is essential that the parent plant is healthy as any disease will be passed on to the new plants. It is also possible to produce new hybrids of your own by crossing two different lilies.

### GROWING LILIES FROM SEED

**1** Fill 10cm (4in) pots with seed compost (soil mix) and a little fine grit. Use ericaceous compost (soil mix) for lilies that will not tolerate lime. Moisten the compost (soil mix) by misting it, or by standing the pot in water. Drain the pots before sowing.

**2** Sow the seed thinly on the surface of the compost (soil mix).

## Seed

Most species set copious seed. Detach the seed capsules from the parent plant when they are fully dry and just beginning to split open, usually towards the end of summer or in early autumn. The seed is best sown fresh, but it can be stored dry over winter in paper envelopes in a cool, dark place for sowing the following spring. While germination can occur within a few weeks, some species are slow and seedlings may not emerge until the second season after sowing. In frost-prone areas, keep the containers in a cold frame over winter.

**3** Cover the seed with fine grit, and leave in a cool, sheltered spot.

**4** After two or three years, the young lilies should be large enough to pot on.

**5** Empty the contents of the pot and carefully separate the bulbs.

**6** Pot up the young bulbs individually and grow them on.

## PROPAGATING LILIES BY BULBLETS

During the growing season, water the seedlings regularly and feed with a liquid fertilizer. Pot them on annually in spring in fresh compost (soil mix), using ericaceous compost (soil mix) for lime-hating species. Most will reach flowering size in three to five years after sowing, when they can be planted out in the garden. Some species are variable, and the new plants may not be identical to the parent.

## Bulblets

Many lilies, both species and hybrids, produce bulblets on the portion of stem below ground. Dig up the lilies towards the end of summer, and detach any bulblets. Pot them up individually in loam-based compost (soil mix) or ericaceous compost (soil mix), covering them to their own depth. Top-dress with grit. Over-winter the bulblets in a cold frame or sheltered spot. When in active growth, feed and water them well. Pot on each spring until they reach flowering size, usually after two to three years.

## Division

Lift the lilies towards the end of summer, and detach any new bulbs that have formed around the basal

**1** Dig up the lily towards the end of the growing season, and check for the presence of bulblets.

**2** Snap off each bulblet, taking care not to damage its roots (see inset). Replant the parent bulb.

**3** Half-fill a 7.5cm (3in) pot with compost (soil mix), and set the bulblet in the centre. Cover to its own depth with compost (soil mix).

**4** Top-dress with grit, then place the pot in a cold frame or sheltered spot to overwinter.

plate. You may need to cut them free with a clean, sharp knife. Replant the parent bulb, and pot up the new bulbs as for bulblets.

## Bulbils

The tiger lily (*L. lancifolium*) and some other species are readily increased by stem bulbs – pea-sized bulbils that form in the leaf axils. Snap them off in late summer, and pot them up in trays of loam-based or ericaceous compost (soil mix), covering them with their own depth of compost (soil mix). Top-dress with grit, and overwinter them in a cold frame or sheltered spot. Treat as for bulblets or seed – they should reach flowering size in two to three years.

## PROPAGATING LILIES BY SCALING

**1** Put some fungicidal powder in a clear plastic bag.

**2** Take a clean, dormant lily bulb and snap off some outer scales, as close to the base as possible.

**3** Put the scales in the bag, and gently shake to coat them with fungicide.

**4** Prepare a mixture of equal parts peat (or an alternative) and perlite or vermiculite in a clear, plastic bag. Dampen the mix. Shake the scales free of excess fungicide, and place them in the bag (see inset).

**5** Blow up the bag, seal it, and label clearly. Keep the bag in a dark place with a mean temperature of 21°C (70°F).

## Scaling

Scaling is more complicated than the previous four methods, but can be used for all lilies. Bulbs can be scaled at any point during the dormant season. Dig up the bulbs and clean them. Snap off as many scales as are needed. Either remove the outer ones only and replant the parent, or scale the whole bulb. Treat the scales with fungicide to prevent infection, then place them in a plastic bag containing a damp, inert mixture of peat (or an alternative) and perlite or vermiculite. Keep the scales in a warm, dark place.

Tiny bulbs should form around the base of each scale within two to three months. When they have developed good root systems, remove the scales from the bag and snap the young bulbs free. Pot them up as for bulblets. Stock from autumn scaling is best kept under glass during the first winter. Note that scaling demands scrupulous hygiene.

## Hybridizing

Hybridization is a sexual method of producing new plants. Lily breeding is a simple process, since the reproductive parts are readily accessible. As with the majority of flowering plants, lilies have flowers with both male and female gametes. To produce fertile seed, pollen, borne on the stamens (male) of one flower, is brought into contact with the stigma (female) of another. Seed develops in the ovary below the stigma.

Lilies that belong to the same division (see Botany and classification) are more likely to set fertile seed when crossed, but it is worth crossing members from different divisions to introduce new characteristics into the group. Commercial trends include the breeding of Asiatic lilies with good scent, and the reduction of scent in lilies for the cut flower trade.

## HYBRIDIZING LILIES

**1** Select a flower on the seed parent that has just opened and cut off the anthers to prevent self-pollination.

**2** Leave the central style intact.

**3** Select the pollen parent, and gather some of its pollen from the anthers with a clean paintbrush.

**4** Brush the pollen onto the sticky surface of the stigma.

**5** After the tepals drop, the ovary containing the seeds begins to swell.

**6** When the ripened seed case splits open, the seed is ready to sow.

Seedlings will share some characteristics with both parents, without being identical to either. Some varieties make better pollen parents than seed parents, and vice versa, so in any breeding programmes it is worth making the cross in both directions. In recording crosses, the convention is to cite the seed parent first, so label the seedlings, for example,

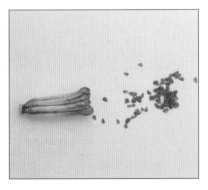

**7** Remove the seedhead from the plant, and gently shake it to release the seed.

'Star Gazer' x 'Casa Blanca', or 'Casa Blanca' x 'Star Gazer', depending on which way you made the cross.

When the seed is ripe, sow it as normal (see Growing lilies from seed). When the seedlings flower, select the best. Back-cross any outstanding seedlings with either of the original parents to consolidate any desirable feature that has been inherited.

# Pests, diseases and other problems

Lilies are prone to a number of problems, whether grown in the open garden or in containers. As with all plants, maintain good hygiene to limit serious damage. Clear away around the lilies any fallen leaves in the autumn, or indeed other debris that might harbour fungal spores, or provide a nesting site for slugs. Good air movement around the lilies will deter aphids that spread viruses.

In addition there are some problems that affect lilies only. All are more or less susceptible to virus, but some manage to survive even though affected. Seriously affected plants should be dug up and destroyed. Do not replant the area with lilies, since many diseases are soil-borne and the virus will persist in the ground for several years. Most species show good disease-resistance, provided their cultivation needs are met, but *L. auratum, L. lancifolium, L. mackliniae,* and *L. sargentiae* are susceptible.

Increasingly, organic controls are available, but not to treat viruses. When applying a proprietary fungicide or pesticide always follow the manufacturer's instructions closely, and wear any protective clothing recommended. Dilute the product as indicated: using excess amounts does not benefit the plant, and may even be toxic to it.

Systemic insecticides do not kill on contact but are taken up by the plant, and then ingested by the pest. The effect is not immediate, therefore, and repeated applications are generally necessary. The following are the most likely problems to be encountered.

## Aphids

*How to identify:* The commonest aphid to attack lilies is greenfly, a tiny green insect visible on the stems and leaves.
*Cause:* Poor garden hygiene; also growing lilies in proximity to other plants, such as roses, that attract the pest.
*Control:* Spray with a proprietary insecticide once you notice an infestation, and repeat as necessary. There are some insecticides available that are selective and leave beneficial insects, such as ladybirds, unharmed.

## Blind shoots

*How to identify:* Flower buds fail to develop.
*Cause:* Usually a check to growth, which may be the result of a viral or pest attack, lack of water and nutrients, or an unexpected, late cold spell.
*Control:* None possible. Blind shoots are a physiological phenomenon and do not necessarily indicate that the bulb is unhealthy.

## Botrytis

*How to identify:* The lower leaves turn brown.
*Cause:* A fungus, encouraged by overcrowding that results in poor air circulation and excessive humidity round the plants.
*Control:* Remove and burn affected leaves to prevent the spread of the fungus. Spray plants with a systemic fungicide. As soon as possible, dig up the lilies and thin them to prevent a recurrence of the problem in future years. Seriously affected plants are best destroyed and replaced with healthy new stock.

Aphids

Blind shoots

The effects of botrytis

## Lily beetle

*How to identify:* Leaves and flowers are eaten. Both adult beetle and larva cause damage. The adult beetle is brilliant scarlet with black head and legs; the larvae are

**Lily beetle damage**

fleshy and greyish-white and resemble bird droppings. Lily beetles are active from early spring to mid-autumn. Another beetle which might attack your lilies is the vine weevil. Vine weevils are a fairly common pest for lily growers.
*Cause:* Warm, dry conditions that favour the pest. The problem is less prevalent in cooler, northern gardens. Fritillaries can also be affected by lily beetles.
*Control:* Remove the insects by hand and dispose of

them; apply a systemic insecticide, such as permethrin, pirimiphos-methyl or fenitrothion and repeat as necessary.

## Rabbits, hares, deer and mice

*How to identify:* Fresh, young growth, the most palatable, is eaten down to ground level; the bulbs themselves may be dug up and eaten. Mice will also eat bulbs stored in garden sheds or outbuildings.
*Cause:* Inadequate protection.
*Control:* For maximim protection, erect a barrier around the garden. To deter rabbits and hares, this should be sunk about 30–45cm (12–18in) into the ground and be 1m (40in) high. A height of at least 2m (6ft) is necessary to keep out deer. Alternatively, surround the bulbs themselves with cylinders of chicken wire, sunk 15cm (6in) into the ground with up to 75cm (30in) above the soil surface. Set rodent traps or use poisoned bait in sheds, or wherever the bare bulbs are stored. Various chemical sprays and dusts are available that deter some mammals, but their effect is temporary and repeated applications are necessary.

## Slugs

*How to identify:* Leaves and stems are eaten at an early stage of growth, while still tender; silvery trails on the soil surface indicate slug activity.
*Cause:* Poor garden hygiene;

**Slug pellets**

lilies growing near paving or among rocks that harbour slugs are particularly susceptible.
*Control:* As new growth emerges in the spring, mulch with grit to provide a surface that the slugs find difficult to negotiate. Regularly check the bases of containers, and dispose of any slugs that shelter there. Slugs can also be poisoned with slug pellets, or by watering liquid metaldehyde around the emerging growth. Biological control is available in the

form of a parasitic nematode that the slugs ingest.

## Viruses

*How to identify:* Leaves and stems are streaked; the whole plant becomes distorted;

**A flower affected by a virus**

flowers are deformed or fail to open properly.
*Cause:* Any of a number of viruses, including cucumber mosaic virus, tulip breaking virus and brown ring virus. They are spread by aphids.
*Control:* Check for and destroy aphid infestations. To prevent the spread of disease wear disposable plastic gloves or, after handling infected bulbs, wash your hands thoroughly before touching other plants. Destroy badly affected plants and replace with new stock.

# Calendar

## Spring

Prepare the ground and plant new bulbs. Mulch existing plantings with well-rotted farmyard manure, garden compost or leaf mould. Top-dress lilies in containers. Pot up young bulbs propagated in previous seasons; plant them out if

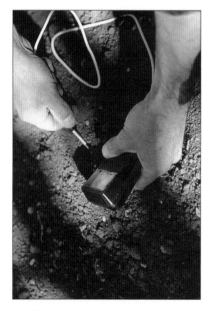

**An electronic meter gives an instant indication of soil acidity/alkalinity.**

they have reached flowering size. As new growth begins, watch out for slugs and kill them. Control greenfly infestations. In rural areas, erect barriers to deter rabbits, hares, deer and mice.

## Summer

Tie in lilies to their stakes as they grow. Water and feed lilies in containers. Hybridize lilies to produce new varieties. Watch out for and control lily beetles, both adults and larvae. Remove bulbils from *L. lancifolium* and others as they form.

**Taller lilies may need tying to stakes as they grow.**

## Autumn

Prepare the ground and plant new bulbs. Dig up and thin out any lilies that have become overcrowded. Lift lilies for propagation; remove

**Soil preparation is essential for good growth and flowering.**

offsets and bulbils, or scale the parent bulb. Gather seed and sow immediately, or store for sowing the following spring.

## Winter

In cold areas, wrap containers loosely with hessian (burlap) or other permeable material, or move the containers into a sheltered spot. Open cold frames containing young bulbs during mild weather. Periodically mist with a fungicide any bare bulbs that are being stored for planting in spring. Set traps or bait for mice.

# Other recommended lilies

Besides the lilies illustrated in the Plant Catalogue, the following are recommended. The number in parentheses after the plant name refers to the lily's division – see Botany and classification. The height given is the maximum the lily can be expected to achieve.

'**All In**' (**7b**)  Hybrid lily with fragrant, bowl-shaped flowers in mid-summer; tepals are white, shaded with soft pink. 1m (40in).

*L. amabile* var. *luteum*  (**9**) Species lily from Korea, with small, unpleasantly scented, turkscap flowers in summer; tepals are yellow, spotted with dark purple. 90cm (3ft).

'All In'

'**Baby Love**' (**7b**)  Hybrid lily with fragrant, bowl-shaped flowers in mid- to late summer; tepals are white with yellow bases. 35cm (14in).

'**Black Beauty**' (**7d**)  Hybrid lily with fragrant, turkscap flowers in mid-summer; tepals are dark red with green base and white margins. 2m (6ft).

*L. amabile* var. *luteum*

'**Black Dragon**' (**6a**)  Hybrid lily with fragrant, trumpet-shaped flowers in early summer; tepals are white with dark purple-red reverse. 1.5m (5ft).

'**Brandywine**' (**1b**)  Hybrid lily with scentless, bowl-shaped flowers in mid-summer; tepals are deep orange with red spots. 1m (40in).

'**Bright Star**' (**6b**)  Hybrid lily with large, fragrant, bowl-shaped flowers in mid- and late summer; tepals are ivory white, banded with orange. 1.5m (5ft).

*L. brownii* var. *viridulum* (**9**) Species lily from China, with large, outward-facing, fragrant, trumpet-shaped flowers in summer; tepals are white,

tinged yellow-green. 1.2m (4ft). Prefers acid soil.

*L. bulbiferum* (**9**)  Species lily (Orange lily) from southern Europe, with scentless, upward-facing, bowl-shaped flowers in early to mid-summer; tepals are orange-red, darker at the base and tip, spotted black or maroon. 1.5m (5ft).

*L. cernuum* (**9**)  Species lily (Nodding lily) from Russia to Korea, with fragrant, turkscap flowers in early and mid-summer; tepals are lilac, pink, purple or, occasionally, white, with purple spots. 60cm (2ft). It is lime-tolerant but is best in acid soil.

'Baby Love'

*L. chalcedonicum* (**9**)  Species lily (Scarlet turkscap lily) from northern Greece and Albania, with unpleasantly scented, turkscap flowers in mid-summer; tepals are bright red

with papillae at the base. 1.5m (5ft). It tolerates any well-drained soil.

'**Chinook**' (**1a**)  Hybrid lily with unscented, bowl-shaped flowers in early to mid-summer; tepals are pale apricot-yellow. 1.2m (4ft).

'Cosmopolitan'

*L. concolor* (**9**)  Species lily (Morning star lily) from western China, with fragrant, star-shaped flowers in early to mid-summer; tepals are glossy scarlet. 1m (40in). Tolerates any well-drained soil.

'**Corsage**' (**1b**)  Hybrid lily with unscented, star-shaped flowers in mid-summer; tepals are pale pink, white at the base, flushed cream and yellow on the reverse. 1.2m (4ft).

'**Cosmopolitan**' (**7b**)  Hybrid lily with fragrant, bowl-shaped flowers in mid-summer; tepals are clear pink to red. 1m (40in).

*L. davidii* (**9**)  This is a species lily from western China. It has scentless, turkscap flowers in summer; tepals are shining vermilion-orange, spotted black. 1.5m (5ft). It is best grown in humus-rich soil.

**L. davidii**

*L. davidii* var. *willmottiae* (**9**) Rhizomatous lily from China, with unscented, turkscap flowers in summer; tepals are vermilion, spotted with purple. 2m (6ft). Tolerates any well-drained soil.

'**Destiny**' (**1a**)  Hybrid lily with scentless, bowl-shaped flowers in early summer; tepals are yellow with brown spots. 1.2m (4ft).

*L. duchartrei* (**9**)  A species lily from China, with fragrant, turkscap flowers in summer; tepals are white, spotted deep purple, flushed purple outside. 1m (40in). Grow in well-drained soil in a cool, shady situation.

'**Fire King**' (**1b**)  Hybrid lily with scentless, funnel-shaped flowers in mid-summer; tepals are bright orange, spotted purple. 1.2m (4ft).

'**Full Time**' (**8**)  Hybrid lily with large, fragrant, bowl-shaped flowers in early summer; tepals are soft salmon-orange. 80cm (32in).

'**Gibralter**' (**1a**)  Hybrid lily with scentless, bowl-shaped flowers in early summer; tepals are bright orange, spotted black. 1m (40in).

'**Dream**'

**Gold Dwarf** (**1a**)  Hybrid lily with bowl-shaped, upward-facing, scentless flowers in early summer; tepals are orange-yellow. 40cm (16in).

**Golden Splendor Group** (**6a**) Hybrid lilies with fragrant, trumpet- to bowl-shaped flowers in mid-summer; tepals are various shades of yellow, banded deep red outside. 2m (6ft).

'**Green Dragon**' (**6a**)  Hybrid lily with fragrant, trumpet-shaped flowers in mid-summer; tepals are white, yellow at the base and flushed greeny-brown outside. 2.1m (7ft).

'**Full Time**'

*L. hansonii* (**9**)  Species lily from eastern Siberia, Korea and Japan with fragrant, turkscap flowers in early summer; tepals are orange-yellow, spotted purple-brown at the base. 1.5m (5ft). Grow in well-drained soil in partial shade.

'**Half Moon**' (**1a**)  Hybrid lily with bowl-shaped, upward-facing, scentless flowers in early summer; tepals are pale creamy-yellow. 40cm (16in).

'**Imperial Gold**' (**7c**)  Hybrid lily with fragrant, star-shaped flowers in late summer; tepals are white, striped yellow centrally. 2m (6ft).

'**Journey's End**' (**7d**)  Hybrid lily with scentless, turkscap flowers in late summer; tepals are deep pink, margined with white, and maroon spots. 2m (6ft).

'**Joy**' (**syn.** '**Le Rêve**'; **7b**) A hybrid lily with scentless, bowl-shaped flowers in mid-summer. The tepals are reddish-purple, and spotted with maroon. 80cm (32in).

'**King Pete**' (**1b**)  Hybrid lily with scentless, bowl-shaped flowers in mid-summer; tepals are cream, generously spotted purple. 1m (40in).

'**Gold Dwarf**'

'**Lady Bowes Lyon**' (**1c**) Hybrid lily with scentless, turkscap flowers in mid-summer; tepals are brilliant red. 1.2m (4ft).

'Lake Toya' (1a) Hybrid lily with bowl-shaped, upward-facing, scentless flowers in early summer. 90cm (3ft).

'Half Moon'

*L. lancifolium* (syn. *L. tigrinum*; 9) Species lily (Tiger lily) from eastern China, Korea and Japan, with scentless, turkscap flowers in late summer to early autumn; tepals are orange, spotted deep purple. 1.5m (5ft). Tolerates some lime but best in acid soil.

*L. lankongense* (9) Species lily from western China, with scented, turkscap flowers in mid- to late summer; tepals are rose-pink, spotted maroon-purple. 1.2m (4ft). Needs cool, moist, lime-free soil.

L. leichtlinii 'Iwashimizu' (9) Selection of a species from Japan, with turkscap flowers in summer; tepals are light yellow, spotted with maroon. Best in lime-free soil in sun or partial shade.

*L. leucanthemum* var. *centifolium* (9) Species lily from western China, with outward-facing, fragrant, funnel- to trumpet-shaped flowers in summer; tepals are white, marked with yellow at the base. 3m (10ft). Tolerates lime.

'Limelight' (6a) Hybrid lily with fragrant, trumpet-shaped flowers in mid-summer; tepals are greeny-yellow, flushed green. 2m (6ft).

'Lake Toya'

'Little Girl' (7b) Hybrid lily with fragrant, bowl-shaped flowers in late summer and early autumn; tepals are rose-pink, spotted crimson. 45cm (18in).

*L. mackliniae* (9) Species lily from north-east India, with scentless, bowl-shaped flowers in late spring to summer; tepals are rose-pink, flushed purple. 60cm (2ft). Grow in humus-rich soil in semi-shade; prone to virus.

L.leichtlinii 'Iwashimizu'

'Magic Pink' (7b) Hybrid lily with lightly scented, bowl-shaped flowers in mid-summer; tepals are soft pink, darker towards the base. 1.2m (4ft).

'Manhattan' (8) Hybrid lily with large, bowl-shaped flowers in early summer; tepals are clear red. 80cm (32in).

*L. medeloides* (9) Species lily from eastern Siberia, north China, Korea and Japan, with scentless, turkscap flowers in mid-summer; tepals are apricot to orange-red, usually with darker spots. 75cm (30in). Needs acid soil in partial shade.

*L. monadelphum* (9) Species lily from north-east Turkey and the Caucasus, with fragrant, trumpet-shaped flowers in early summer; tepals are yellow, spotted purple or maroon, flushed purple-brown outside. 1.5m (5ft). Tolerates lime.

'Montreux' (1a) Hybrid lily with scentless, cup-shaped flowers in mid-summer; tepals are pink, spotted with brown at the base. 1m (40in).

'Mrs R.O. Backhouse' (2) Hybrid lily with scentless, turkscap flowers in summer; tepals are orange-yellow, sparsely spotted brown, flushed yellow on the reverse. 2m (6ft).

*L. leucanthemum* var. *centifolium*

*L. nanum* (9) Species lily from the Himalayas and western China, with fragrant, bell-shaped flowers in early summer; tepals vary from pale pink to purple. 30cm (1ft).

Needs acid soil and partial shade.

**Olympic hybrids (6a)** Hybrid lilies with fragrant, trumpet-shaped flowers in mid- to late summer; tepals vary in colour but are usually white, sometimes shaded green on the reverse. 2m (6ft).

'Manhattan'

**'Partner' (1a)** Hybrid lily with bowl-shaped, upward-facing, scentless flowers in early summer; tepals are clear red. 40cm (16in).

**Pink Perfection group (6a)** Hybrid lilies with fragrant, trumpet-shaped flowers in mid-summer; tepals are pale pink to deep fuchsia pink. 2m (6ft).

**'Pirate' (1a)** Hybrid lily with scentless, star-shaped flowers in early summer; tepals are brilliant orange-red. 1.2m (4ft).

*L. pomponium* **(9)** A species lily from the French and Italian Alps, with unpleasantly scented, turkscap flowers in early to mid-summer; tepals are bright scarlet, spotted with black, flushed purple-green outside. 1m (40in). Prefers alkaline soil.

*L. pumilum* **(9)** Species lily from Siberia to Mongolia, northern China and northern Korea, with scented, turkscap flowers in early summer; tepals are scarlet, sometimes spotted black. 45cm (18in). Needs acid soil.

'Partner'

*L. rubellum* **(9)** Species lily from Japan, with fragrant, funnel-shaped flowers in early summer; tepals are rose-pink, sometimes spotted with maroon at the base. 80cm (32in). Needs acid soil and partial shade.

*L. sargentii* **(9)** Species lily from western China, with fragrant, trumpet-shaped flowers in mid- to late summer; tepals are white with yellow bases, flushed green or purple outside. 1.5m (5ft). Needs lime-free soil in full sun.

*L. speciosum* var. *magnificum*

**'Sterling Star' (1a)** Hybrid lily with slightly scented, bowl-shaped flowers in early to mid-summer; tepals are white, spotted brown. 1.2m (4ft).

*L. superbum* **(9)** Species lily (American turkscap lily) from eastern USA, with scentless, turkscap flowers in late summer to early autumn; tepals are orange flushed with red, spotted maroon, with green bases. 3m (10ft). Prefers acid soil.

*L.* x *testaceum* **(3)** Hybrid lily (Nankeen lily), a cross

between *L. candidum* and *L. chalcedonicum*, with fragrant, turkscap flowers in early to mid-summer; tepals are pale apricot-pink, lightly spotted red. 1.2m (4ft). Tolerates lime.

**'Wall Street' (8)** Hybrid lily with large, bowl-shaped flowers in early summer; tepals are deep red. 90cm (3ft).

*L. wilsonii* **(9)** Species lily from Japan, with large, upward-facing, unscented, bowl-shaped flowers in summer; tepals are orange-red, striped yellow at the base and spotted with dark brown-red. 1m (40in). Needs well-drained soil in sun or partial shade.

'Wall Street'

**Yellow Blaze group (1a)** Hybrid lilies with scentless, bowl-shaped flowers in mid- to late summer; tepals are bright yellow, spotted reddish-brown. 1.5m (5ft).

# Index

## ACKNOWLEDGEMENTS

The author and publishers would like to thank: Bruce Robertson, Cairngrow Lilies, Rait; and Peter Schenk, Bischoff Tulleken Lelies, Wieringerwerf, Holland. For photographs used in the book: Christine Skelmersdale for the use of the photographs on pages 22t, 23t, 24b, 27b, 28t, 28b, 33b, 35t, 35b, 39t, 39b; the Harry Smith Picture Library for page 56l; Peter McHoy for page 57l.